Pink Lace

Cover, title page and other photos by Douglas C. Granum.

Cover design by Scott Norris. Painting by Douglas C. Granum

douglasgranum.com | monkeyhouse-media.com

ISBN 978-1-939723-17-8

First Edition

PINK LACE

DOUGLAS C. GRANUM

POEMS

Salmon Girl & The Scent of Love

My sleek silver darling I don't know the surging rivers, creeks,
trenches of the seas of our saline love by name,
I know them by your heady scent,
returning King Salmon, sensing rivers shallow, sun shad-
owed, creek beds, you returning from the sea.
I anticipate your smoothness, wetness, silkiness, your slipperi-
ness, so long so tantalizing.
There is the touch of your nose, sea polished , hard insistent,
your feathering gills, blood infused.
Your cloud-like fins, caressing each part of me, I involuntarily
give up melt.
Your sweeping body, your turgid tail
You touch me in a thousand different ways and at each electric
caress I spurt golden eggs.
When you touch me,
I am lost then discovered, we have returned
from our oceanic quest.
My torn fins cradling you
My senses filled with your scent in the crescent of your elegant
green polished speckled back
You are mine alone beneath our creeks autumnal
voluptuous watery world.
There are mosses and stones with memory,
There are alder trees and ferns nurtured by the bones and flesh
of our ancient ancestors lining the creek banks.

Around us twisting currents carry gnats, small twigs, leaves,
these currents move us while we kiss.
We slowly swim while you thrusting playfully, me coyly
swimming up under a green moss log pretending to hide.
We are carried along on the jade silk current, sometimes side-
ways, over the brown tessellated pebbled bottom.
My pave' silver scales, my glowing electric lateral line,
You know that place.
Touch it,
its Electric!
Your head resting on my shoulder
We adore each other. Sunlight filters through the green tea
creek waters, small grasses waver in the
dapped underwater light.
My tail is ragged, my bones show through my skin for I too
swam from the fathomless ocean, up rivers and creeks. I eddy,
here in the current.
I hover here resting feeling my egg sacks growing.
I position my waiting, disintegrating flesh, for your arrival, I
am open.
My gold colored tiger torn striped decaying body is flagellated
from sticks and sharp rocks.
Above the creeks surface, mist turns to wind in the high firs,
the wind causes a rain of dry fir needles to fall above us on the
river's surface, our sky.
Different kinds of rain drops dot the river.
I watch as you come gaping to the surface rain splashing off
the surface of your shinny powerful nose
grabbing a floating fly.

Crystal creeks run in torrents through the forest. It is autumn,
golden leaves drift over us.
You swam to me.
How I loved you at that moment,
You emerging from the slanting sunlit water emerging at the
end of your journey, then a quick frothing thrust of your pow-
erful tail and you are next to me,
I feel your electricity in the whole creek.
I made ready our gravel bed.
Can every moment in this life be unique?
We kiss, taste of deep ocean, God the surging of
blood through my gills.
Salty, alive, magic, sensual waves, you, you sleek King, cause
me to spontaneously drop eggs!
Crushing on the shores of our desires
Retreating down stream into the rapids, then thrashing turn-
ing racing back up stream again.
We play, we court, we swirl the creek, we ambush, leave wakes
while running up to a small quiet sunlit pool, a place beneath
a revered ancient alder, an exact place, where years ago we
drifted as pink eggs with large glaucous blue eyes.
Closing my eyes, I feel the riverine landscape of your back,
your fins, your rasping, your vibrant thrusts, the swirl of milt
and eggs, ivory and gold,
Birth, such a draining.
I feel your river wet lips seeking mine,
In your saline oceanic scent I seek your fresh water source.
From icy sea primal ocean, you returned to me, my silver
darling.

You smelling of deep Aleutian trenches, of profundity and Kamchatka currents, the great clockwise swirling north pacific scents of the rivers of the Russian taiga.
From somewhere out there you found me waiting here in my quiet sun dappled pool.
You came powering thrashing up rapids finally gliding into my quiet still pool, over the old water logged mossy log, I saw you jump, I have been waiting,
I roll,
flutter my pink pearl labia
Sliding beneath your surface
I willingly lose sight of life
Drifting with natal currents
I don't think, I don't know, blindly desiring,
I only remember the scent of alder laced earth and wild rose,
Sunlight radiating off of your silver magnificence,
Around us great comforting boulders, above the surface trees with blue sky wavering in the river current's surface.
Primeval blood scents of female drift on the river's menstrual currents,
I feel strong, I can thrust, I accept.
I have done what I came to do.
A fin brushes me,
Seeks me
Pulling me to the surface
Was I diving or am I dying?
Or was that a dream, did you swim to me?
There is moss, forest, earth
A pebble bed in a sunny stream

I shudder, I shake Ivory skeins of eggs,
my body is sex.
Your glacial blue eyes find me
Awakened with your reflected heat,
That tantalizing distant roar must be our ocean
Calling me home on the ebbing tide.

Passionate Sun

A lily pale, softly scented
Clad in white yet red

A fragrant portal with diaphanous petals embracing passionate sun
Above this flower a new crescent moon hangs waiting

Madly in seasons desires
Gathering moistures moments at your portals

There lies a bower of bent spring grass
Beneath flowering cherries, pink, where two lovers lay embracing

Consider this setting for a moment
Nurtured by all outdoors,

Pendulous peaches, lips, jasmine blossoms
Perfume of old fashion rose, an edible garden dark and earthy

Fields in May where flowers grow,
children run

A secret nook inside the lily, a place of honey bees and birds
Where joy is constant and love is sure

While nectar pulses the lilies stem
We once more sink on springs grasses.

An innocent cup of coffee?

In the meeting of two personalities
Or contact of two chemical substances
If any reaction occurs
Both are forever transformed.

Consider it original Joy

Love is hard to come by
Love is of the heart

Love is the shadow cast by a friend
Anywhere you go your friendship follows you behind the sun

Search for love
Love is trust

Love is eye to eye intimate
Love is the hope of intimacy

Love is hope
Hoping for love is pain

Finding love is a surprise
True love is attainable

Love is ever changing
Can I say this about our love: I want to be with you all the time.

Love is our desire
I love your desire of me, I treasure my desire of you

Cradle me in this life, let me hold you
I live for you, your kisses, your embraces

The sound of your voice
To watch you smile

Castello di Oliveto,
Montespertoli, Italy.

An Unexpected Gift

Consider it Joy
An unexpected gift,
A deserved bonus,
A little something extra for my heart.
Oh, your love does fill my heart with joy
A joy that could fill a forest; every sunlit tree its evidence.

Why then, do I wake, my heart a rain drenched windowpane,
my mind a
Whirling weathervane, longing at least to hear your name?
Rest, I say.
Think of twinkling lights on the far side of dark water.
How would it be?
How dark, cold, and lonely would I feel if those lights died
out?
Let them twinkle. Let them burn. Embrace this love.
Consider it joy!

Our Moment to Flourish

This moment, is our moment to flourish
How resplendent you are.

Let me hold you
Study you, admire you.

Our eternity is this brilliant moment
I wish for it never to pass

When I stare deeply at you
I am awakened with a sense of awe

Something reveals itself in you to me
That something surpasses my understanding.

Beauties hidden in ancient patterns
Infinite and intangible

A slight parting of your lips
Warmth in your smile

Strength in your bearing
Voluptuous in your movements

How little I know
Yet somehow, I feel I have known you forever

Oh, my love gently, close your eyes
Join me in this kiss, feel our lips touch

I know you are mine

Since our extraordinary first moment
I have thought of no one else

I know I have no right to you
But then I have no right to the clouds either

I know I have no right to you
Yet I hear rain on the roof and think of you

Though you are not beside me
Cherry trees still blossom and green grass grows beneath them

There are no answers
For our happiness at sunrise or flowers in your garden

Can there be words
For young falling alder leaves

Or love at that perfect moment
When soul mates touch

Searching for your scent
I find it in the storm winds off the sea

I discover your luminous aura
Standing sunlit in the forest, somewhere in a dream

I see myself in a dream as a young boy smiling
Watching us together we are happy

I know I have no right to you
Yet in the heart of this universe I know you are mine

"I love you because I know no other way"

Love Changes Everything

Walking naked at night my feet cool on our cottage floor
I dream of your moist breath, your tongue touching my ear,
a caress.
I am wearing nothing
I want feel your enthusiasm sweeping through me.
Walking nude, I feel you
here, there, here and yes, even there.
I am filling the house with scented red flowers, I have lighted
candles, I rang my small bell to attract you.
I watch vermillion metal sunrises, edged with
cobalt and Safire.
Lightly resting on my quivering imagination,
I Taste gentle first intoxications of love, while brushing your
lips with mine, they tickle.
In my hands and my thoughts there is inspired virtuosity,
My hands roam, they know my tender body best
When you arrived in my soul
Did you whisper something to me then or was it a look,
or was it chance?
Is it so easy to fall in love?
Did you dare so much, did I?
Was it written on the life line of your palm?
What I tried to explain
Seemed unexplainable.
Was there music?
Love changes everything

My Eager Lover

My eager lover is coming to me.
I am waiting by my window to catch a first glimpse of her.
She will be smiling; her eyes will be shining.
I will feel, for I know myself, I will feel breathless.
I am already excited.

Slate-hard cold-rain falls,
Threading her lithe body, my lover, my darling,
through the gust driven rain,
Insistent assaulting winter drops falling on her heated
finely molded face,
she will have walked a long way to see me
When she arrives, I will gently remove her soaking hat, I will
kiss her cold salty lips, press her fridged wet face against mine.
give her sweet Turkish coffee, warm her hands against my
chest, I will open my shirt.
But know this, she is coming.
She isn't here yet,
But, I know she is coming
She does love me, she told me so.

Walking through the dripping forest, I wonder
Can see my candles burning?

Will she see me, through my rain drenched window, at my
table pretending to be writing.

Waiting seems so long,

history is the future.

Wait, I'm laughing now, for I am sure, is that her I see weaving
through the trees?
Her small feet in high boots, she is avoiding puddles.
Or no, this hurts it's only a fern waving in the wind, not yet,
she isn't coming yet,
it is just my overwhelming desire and eagerness
tricking and playing little jokes with me.

Maybe she won't come, please not that.
It is blowing harder now, no matter how I try to pretend, the
rain, the endless rain hammering
Sideways against the windows
falling water dances across the cove.
Rain drops out of dull pewter skies onto pewter water,
Then popping back up like small clear figurines, to fall once
more. I must admit the weather is ugly

She will come though, she is coming, she told me she would,
when she says she is coming she comes..
She is as eager as I,
My eager lover.

The candles burn lower
They lick and flicker little wavering red tongues of heat.
As I watch them, hot and molten, a little red melting
tear of wax
Breaks over the rim of one and slowly, ever so slowly,
runs red down the shaft, while at the same time a small tear
runs down my cheek into the corner of my lip.

Quieted by Nature's Hand

Dearest it is snowing again
My heart rises to silk flakes each flake, like you, unique

Tumbling serenely hypnotically while watching you
I drift silent as thought, a white owl

Islands snow-dark, mystic
I love these islands you come to mind, mysterious

Hushed lagoon, drifting snow, so quiet
A chortling loon, my thoughts separate.

As always with you, first blond, then blue then smiling
Then goodness, then anxiety.

Reflecting black, white, on hushed waters,
The loon again loon calls

Over on the island, valleys dark as thighs,
Fill with slanting white cool snow

Quieted by nature's hand
Our dogs' slumber in the heat of the fireplace where I held you
last night, no lace.

My fingers explore the piano, I paint flowers
Dreaming in the falling snow of you

In my rainy garden autumns apples hang red simple and complete
And, like you, magic thrives in their being

Their innocence belies their complexity
They are questions without answers.

I love you because I know no other way

Today a woman's love is a whiter winter rose.
Dear friend it is hypnotically snowing still.

Separated by Lace

In silent
day and night

Our secrets drop
Honeyed tears

Hip to Hip
Heart to heart
Yet still lace apart

A form from memory
Where rain drops fall.

A Purling Brook
An old brass bed

Beside a shallow sunlit stream
Where blood and warmth touch my wing

In this winter garden
Sinking in delight
Beneath your feathered quilt
Your passion is me

We Frolic
We laugh

We thrust,
We kiss each other
Everywhere

Lie still she parts,
Hold still for my sake, don't move,

Sinking in joy we rise on fervent dreams

Sky above, moss beneath,
The roar must be the sea
In the secret of the night.

Where Is Love?

Now war rages
Everywhere frantic people make believe.
Where is there safety?
Where is love?

It is dark, so dark I can't see you
We are standing in the forest
You are laughing your face wet from the warm rain

Your lips find my open collar
Resisting the urge to sink down on the wet moss
I dream the dreams of lovers as your mouth closes on
my ear

My hands will themselves
How long had we known each other?

My eyes couldn't adjust to the dark
Only my lips and hands

Drinking at the well of longing
Finding in your waters, nourishment.

Your eyes over me, your eyes under me
My shadow rests on your belly.

Too Late to Talk

GRANDFATHER, EIGHTY-FIVE, ME EIGHT,
LAY CLOSE IN BED.

GRANDMA KATIE HAD LONG AGO VANISHED
IN A CEREMONY.

I LAY WRAPPED IN THAT LOVING STRONG, coal dusted OLD BLACKSMITH'S ARM in his brass bed talking. I STARed INTO THE DARK void talking WITH GRANDPA, WHILE LISTENING TO THE ENDLESS NORTHWEST RAINS WASHING HIS OLD TARPAPER SHACK.
His tan and green Monarch wood stove had gone out hours ago, the bedroom was black, non-reflective.

WINDS PUSHED, FORCING, BENDING THE HIGH TOPS OF THE FIRS, EVERY NOW AND AGAIN I WOULD HEAR A BRANCH SNAP IN THE WIND, ONCE IN A WHILE A TREE FELL.

THE SAME RUSHING WINDS SWIRLED AND EDDIED
RATTLING HIS LOOSE AND DRAFTY WINDOW.

THE SMALL DARK BEDROOM WAS COLD, THE WOOD STOVE HAD GONE OUT HOURS AGO, THE BEROOM WAS VERY DARK.
THE BED WITH ITS SOFT FLANEL SHEETS, ITS MOUN-

TAINOUS HAND MADE QUILT, WAS ALSO COLD WHEN I MOVED.

I LAY WITH MY HEAD IN GRANDPA'S ARM, RIGHT AS CLOSE AS I COULD GET TO HIM. IT WAS WARM NEAR GRANDFATHER'S MASSIVE SIDE AND I SNUGGLED THERE, a duckling under his loving wing
WE TALKED ABOUT A LOT OF THINGS, WE TALKED ABOUT HIS BLACKSMITH'S SHOP, HOW TO WELD steel IN A FORGE, THE HAMMERED STEEL FISHING SPEARHEAD I WAS GOING TO FORGE IN THE MORNING. Why did the Indians only sharpen their knives on one side?

GRANDPA GOT TO TALKING ABOUT LIFE IN THE COAL MINES OF NORTH DAKOTA AND A BOY I WISH I KNEW. He painted a picture of a mine in Zap, North Dakota, of tumble-down buildings, lumber stacked and unstacked, rail lines in the dusty coal, Steam pipes were spewing white flour like plums of hot steam. Built into the side of a hill, like many early mines on the great plains. Coal shows itself often, some has been burning for a century or more. Early mines were just standing at a coal face out in the open and then following the seam underground. Cables, and coal cars, donkeys and steam shovels, picks and dynamite, carbine lamps and snow-white eye balls on the miners faces in the midst of jet-black faces.

When he stopped talking, I asked him if there were Indians and Buffalo in North Dakota when he was my age?

I murmured into his muscular arm, "why didn't he have any kids?" I was his son he said, this made me feel loved, but then my love for grandfather was boundless. IASKED WHY HE HAD NO KIDS? I WAS HIS son HE SAID, THIS MADE ME FEEL LOVED.

SOMEDAY, HE SAID QUIETLY, I WLL GIVE THIS ALL TO YOU, THE HOUSE, THE GARDEN, THE CHICKEN COOP MY TOOLS AND THE BLACKSMITH'S SHOP.

I asked him if I could have a couple of Grandma Katie's glass eye balls I found rolling around in his cedar chest. Grandma had lost an eye when she was just a young woman, she had four or five glass eye balls that stared out at me every time I opened the cedar chest.

I LAY NOT KNOWING, NOR WONDERING THROUGH TEMPESTUOUS WIND LADENED BLACK RAINY NIGHTS, THAT HE WOULDN'T ALWAY BE THERE BY MY SIDE NEVER OCCURRED TO MY YOUNG MIND.
I didn't know that he wouldn't forever be there by my side. I didn't know at that time that we were both living and dying. It never occurred to my young mind that grandfather lived his life without getting old, he was as young as I was, age wasn't important.

SOMETIMES WE WOULD TALK ABOUT MAKING A NEW PATH THROUGH THE WOODS TO OUR HOUSE. WE TALKED ABOUT WHAT WE WOULD BE HAVING FOR

BREAKFAST, PANCAKES ON THE RANGE TOP I HOPED.

I ASKED HIM WHY HE LEFT BEAULA, NORTH DAKOTA TO COME AND LIVE NEAR US IN SOUTHWORTH. WASN'T MUCH COAL IN SOUTHWORTH, IN FACT NONE THAT I KNEW OF.

I ASKED WHY STEEL TURNS CRYSTALLINE WHEN IT BUBBLES AND Gets CHERRY HOT, could I use baking soda to POLISH MY POP-GEAR, WOULD HE SHOW ME HOW TO SHARPEN MY POCKET KNIFE, HOW COME COWS HAVE four STOMACHS, WHY DO GEESE FLY SOUTH IN THE WINTER WHEN THEY ARE COVERED IN GOOSE DOWN, wouldn't that keep them warm? Did old grandpa Levenseller die on the path to the store? Hey Grandpa bet you didn't know we caught a rat in the trap in the chicken coop. WHY DOES METAL RUST?

Grandpa tell me, would ya MAKE ME FRIED BALONY FOR BREAKFAST WITH PANCAKES, home-made raspberry jam, AND A COUPLE OF EGGS, IF I MAKE your COFFEE? Yes he said and I will make you hot chocolate with baby marshmallows, and Vienna sausages on the side, he knew I loved Vienna sausages,

Yes son, HE CHUCKLED, YES that's a deal.

We lay there awhile me right up close to him, listening to the rattling window and the ceaseless rains assaulting the tar paper roof. Somewhere in the room after the last sudden down pour, I heard water slowly dripping in the dark from the ceiling on the cold linoleum floor.

AFTER A WHILE, I NOTICED I WAS THE ONLY ONE TALKING, Grandpa WASN'T TALKING ANYMORE.

GRANDPA?
Yes?
YOU AWAKE,
I asked?

HE Rumbled AND Coughed A BIT THEN Chuckled IN HIS WARM WAY AND Said YES SON I'M AWAKE.
Why?
Well I just asked if you remember the other day when I rushed into your house, and that old lady was sitting on your knee and was kissin' you, well you didn't say anything, so I was wondering if you were awake, and who was she anyway?

With that he laughed
THEN WHILE TURNING ON HIS SIDE HE PULLED ME CLOSE into his warm spot in THAT DAMP OLD WARM BED, UNDER THOSE LONG-AGO WET WINTERS AND SAID, "IT WAS TOO LATE TO TALK".

Now sleep tight and DON'T LET THE BEDBUGS BITE," he said.

He gave a long quiet broken sigh and then said, "I adore you son more than you will ever know. I heard him kind of choke again on these last words.

Then HE SAID, "I LOVE YOU SON, God do I love you, GOOD NIGHT NOW."

We were quiet for a bit more after he SAID THAT, about "I adore you", He wrapped me even closer and tighter, it was then I felt a hot tear fall on my forehead then run down my cheek.

"GRANDPA, I SAID, YOU CRYING?"

HE DIDN'T SAY ANYTHING, BUT I KNEW HE WASN'T SLEEPING, NOT JUST YET ANYWAY.

AFTER A WHILE WHEN HIS BREATHING STARTED TO EVEN OUT, HE GAVE ME A GOOD HARD SQUEEZE, THEN ROLLED ON HIS OTHER SIDE AND PULLED HIS KNEES UP.

I ROLLED OVER next to his strong back AND STRETCHED MY SMALL THIN white ARM UP AND OVER HIS POWERFUL coal miners BACK.

I WHISPERED INTO THE MASSIVE BULK OF HIS BACK, "I LOVE YOU GRANDPA, and I don't know why but I started to cry, why do we cry?

I LAY THERE sobbing quietly LISTENING TO ALL OF THE

other NIGHT SOUNDS, RAIN SPLASHING UNDER THE EVES, A FROG SOMEWHERE scratching out a love song, a ferry boat's deep whistle out on the sound searching its's way through the foul winds and a hundred kinds of rain.

THEN I heard GRANDPA'S LIGHT SNORING and knew he was sleeping.

I lay there and started thinking about grandpa's world back in North Dakota, that he so often told me about. What a difference from the Pacific Northwest.

I heard the singing songs of the MEADOWLARKS, the eerie sounds of flying geese in high night skies, golden fields of nodding SUN FLOWERS.

I heard the scrapping and screeching quiet sounds of a steel plow pulled by strong horses turning over virgin soil. I thought of pitchy black coal mines, with miners and carbide lamps, wandering, pick in hand, up to an endless coal seam that, goes under states and rivers for hundreds of miles in underground darkness. Their coal dusted dollars, Jurassic prong-horned antelope, cherry colored melting steel, the ring of a hammer on a hand-poured anvil.

I drifted, getting sleepier, I tried to hold on but finally when I thought I was still awake,

I saw the great periwinkle blue skies of North Dakota rising over ranch lands and COAL MINES, buffalo AND ANVILS, picks and shovels. Ducks drifted in dream states on reed lined ponds in reflective moon light, fields of waving wheat stalks bent here and there by small resting singing birds, cows dreamingly placidly grazing.

I lay wrapped in his loving coal miners arm staring with heavy eyes into the dark.

I listen to the hammering endless rains.

It rained, it blew, trees cracked, grandpa snored, the windows rattled, I could hear grandpa's windup alarm clock.

Then nightfall, on the Great Northern Prairies of North Dakota.

Then the soft warm kiss of my mother on my cheek.

Then I slept snuggled up close as I could get to my Grandpa.

Silkflakes

Dear Friend it is snowing now
My heart rises to silk flakes

Tumbling serenely hypnotically
I drift silent as thought, a white owl

Islands snow dark, near seem mysterious
I love them you come to mind

As always with you, first blond, then blue then smiling
Then goodness, then anxious colorful butterflies

Reflecting black white, on hushed waters,
A loon calls, separating my quiet

Over on the island valleys dark as thighs,
Fill with slanting snow

Quieted by heaven
Our dogs sleep in the heat of the fireplace

My fingers explore the piano, I paint flowers
Dreaming in the falling snow of you

In my garden autumns apples hang red simple and complete
And, like you, magic thrives in their being

Their innocence belies their complexity
They are questions without answers.

Today a woman's love is a white winter rose.
Dear friend it is snowing still.

To author and artist Douglas Granum, creation is a way of life.

His inspiration is derived from his travels around the world and an appreciation of the unusual – trekking the jungles of New Guinea, enjoying plein aire painting in northern Urals of Russia, drifting down China's Yangtze River, looking at the stars in a Serengeti night sky, and commercial fishing in the storm-tossed Gulf of Alaska.

As an artist Douglas Granum works with and in various mediums including stone, metal, glass, wood, canvas, bronze and of course, writing. From creation in his studio in Southworth, Washington, his paintings, glass pieces, metal and stone sculptures can be found worldwide.

Find out more at DouglasGranum.com

Other stories by Douglas Granum:

THE ROSE COVERED COTTAGE

THE GERMAN MUSIC TEACHER'S COTTAGE

ALONE ON THE YELLOW STONE

JUDITH'S GAP

WAR NO PEACE

OFF A LIGHT

DEATH AND AFTERLIFE ON EL PASEO

www.ingramcontent.com/pod-product-compliance
Lightning Source LLC
Chambersburg PA
CBHW031258210726
48287CB00003B/1079

* 9 7 8 1 9 3 9 7 2 3 1 7 8 *